LET'S ROCK!

What Are Minerals?

Natalie Hyde

Crabtree Publishing Company

www.crabtreebooks.com

Crabtree Publishing Company

www.crabtreebooks.com

Author: Natalie Hyde

Publishing plan research and development:
Sean Charlebois, Reagan Miller
Crabtree Publishing Company

Project coordinator: Kathy Middleton

Photo research: Tibor Choleva, Melissa McClellan

Design: Tibor Choleva

Editor: Adrianna Morganelli

Proofreaders: Rachel Stuckey, Crystal Sikkens

Production coordinator: Margaret Amy Salter

Prepress technician: Margaret Amy Salter

Print coordinator: Katherine Berti

Geological consultant:
Dr. Kimberly Tait

Cover: pyrite (center); malachite (bottom right); azurite (left)

Title page: Thermal Reserve, Rotorua, New Zealand

This book was produced for Crabtree Publishing Company by BlueAppleWorks.

Photographs and reproductions:

© dreamstime.com: Sikth(4 top), Sergey Lavrentev(4/5 bottom), Natursports(5 top), Sergio Bertino(6 bottom), Zelenka68(8 bottom left), Michal Baranski(9 left large),Gozzoli (9 top left,13{8}), Omkr(9 top right),Domiciano Pablo Romero Franco(9 bottom right),350jb(10/11 large), Del69(10 middle),Paulbroad(10 bottom),Serg_dibrova(11 top),Valpal(11, 2cd from top),Tatiana Morozova(11, 3rd from top),Pavle Marjanovic(12 top), Farbled(13{9}, 21 top left), Nicku(15 bottom left),Amikphoto(16 top), Tomislav Zivkovic(16 middle), Altiso(16 bottom),Rainer Walter Schmied(17 left), Vladimir Vlasov(18 bottom),Domiciano Pablo Romero Franco(22 bottom), Ferenz(22 bottom right),Karol Brandys(24 left,24 right),Paul Fleet(24 bottom),Ron Chapple(25 top left),Frannyanne(25 left),Israel Enrique García Mckee(25 bottom left),Andreas Karelias(25 bottom large), Fedor Kondratenko (26 left),Stevehullphotography(27 middle),Landd09(28 bottom), Galina Ermolaeva(29 right) / © fotolia: Africa Studio(6 right), afitz(14 top), andy koehler(14 middle), FotoGem(14 bottom) / © iStockphoto.com: Ken Tannenbaum(17 top), Kerstin Waurick(28/29 middle), Melissa Carroll(29 top) / © Shutterstock.com: Mirec (cover: center), Natalia Yudenich (cover: bottom right), Pablo Romero (cover: left), Rufous (cover: bottom middle), Steve Reed(background every page), Margrit Hirsch(headline and boxtop), Cloudia Newland(title page, 4 bottom), Grigoryeva Liubov Dmitrievna (5 left),pmphoto(5 bottom right), Anton Balazh(5 large bottom), Tyler Boyes(8 bottom middle, 10 top, 13{6}, 13{5}, 15 top right), AVprophoto(9 middle left), IDAL(9 middle right), Laitr Keiows(9 bottom left), Sergey Lavrentev (9 bottom middle),morrbyte(9 bottom large), MarcelClemens (12 bottom, 13{10}), Manamana(12/13 bottom large,26 right), Fribus Ekaterina(13{7}), Nicholas Sutcliffe(13{4}), Jiri Slama(13{3}), Terry Davis(13{2}, 16 large, 19 top), rehoboth foto(14/15 large), RcpPhoto(17 large), Helen & Vlad Filatov (18/19 large), Sergio Ponomarev (18 top), Jeff Schultes(19 right),Vera Kailova(20/21 large),Michal Baranski(20 bottom),Oleksiy Mark(21 left bottom), gracious_tiger(21 right large),V. J. Matthew(22 top), A.S. Zain(23 top), B Brown(23 middle), iofoto (23 bottom), Juri(24 large), Africa Studio(25 right), Fokin Oleg(25 middle), Rachelle Burnside(26/27 large), Andrei Zarubaika|(27 bottom), Ty Smith(27 right), hjschneider (28 middle), Alex Staroseltsev (28 left) / © Rob Lavinsky, iRocks.com: 15 bottom / © Jason Pineau: 21 top middl / Public Domain: NOAA (7 top), 8 bottom right,11 bottom, 13 bottom right,(13{1}),15 top left, 25 3rd from top, 29 left / © David Brock illustrations: 7 bottom

Library and Archives Canada Cataloguing in Publication

Hyde, Natalie, 1963-
    What are minerals? / Natalie Hyde.

(Let's rock)
Includes index.
Issued also in electronic formats.
ISBN 978-0-7787-7215-6 (bound).--ISBN 978-0-7787-7220-0 (pbk.)

    1. Minerals--Juvenile literature. 2. Mineralogy--Juvenile literature. I. Title. II. Series: Let's rock (St. Catharines, Ont.)

QE365.2.H93 2012   j549   C2012-900252-6

Library of Congress Cataloging-in-Publication Data

CIP available at Library of Congress

Crabtree Publishing Company

www.crabtreebooks.com   1-800-387-7650

Printed in the USA /012014/CG20131129

Published in Canada
Crabtree Publishing
616 Welland Ave.
St. Catharines, Ontario
L2M 5V6

Published in the United States
Crabtree Publishing
PMB 59051
350 Fifth Avenue, 59th Floor
New York, New York 10118

Published in the United Kingdom
Crabtree Publishing
Maritime House
Basin Road North, Hove
BN41 1WR

Published in Australia
Crabtree Publishing
3 Charles Street
Coburg North
VIC 3058

CONTENTS

THE MINERAL WORLD

The ground under our feet is made up of many different solids: sand, soil, rocks, and boulders. Every solid in the ground contains minerals. A mineral is made up of small building blocks called elements. Minerals form in nature, at the bottom of the ocean and on every **continent**.

ATTRACTIVE GRANITES

Rocks are made of minerals and each rock can have a different combination of them. Granites are made up primarily of three minerals: quartz, potassium feldspar, and plagioclase. Granite can range in color, from white-gray to pink, depending how much of each of the three key minerals are present. Granites sometimes have other black minerals in them. Granites are a very attractive rock for countertops and building stones.

▲ Red granite contains feldspar.

▶ Milky quartz is one of the most common varieties of quartz and can be found almost anywhere.

COLORS OF THE RAINBOW

One of the most common minerals that you'll see on Earth is quartz. Quartz is made up of silicon and oxygen and can be almost every color in the rainbow.

▼ Some people use granite for their kitchen countertops.

WHAT DO YOU DO?

❋ Mineralogists are scientists that study minerals. They spend a lot of time in laboratories **analyzing** samples or out in the field in remote areas. People in this branch of geology often study beautiful **gemstones** and precious jewels or work on locating valuable minerals for mining companies.

▼ *A mineralogist studies minerals with a magnifying tool called a loupe.*

EIGHT IS THE NUMBER

There are thousands of minerals in the world and many of them are made up of just eight elements: oxygen, silicon, aluminum, iron, magnesium, calcium, potassium, and sodium.

▼ *A collection of many different minerals*

▼ *Minerals can be found in caves.*

COOL IT!

New minerals are forming every day on Earth's surface, under the oceans, and deep inside Earth. When the right conditions occur, minerals will start to form from the elements that are present in gases or liquids. It takes billions of elements to make up the minerals we see!

PUSHY MAGMA

Magma is the hot liquid rock deep inside Earth. The magma pushes up through Earth's thin outer layer called the crust to form volcanoes. As the magma reaches the surface, it cools, and depending on which elements **bond** together, different minerals form.

▼ *Magma is called lava when it reaches the surface and comes out of a volcano.*

CRYSTALS AND GEMS

Minerals can grow into different crystal shapes with the right conditions. Some minerals form unique crystals. They are called gemstones. When gemstones are cut and polished, they are called **gems**. Gems are used to make jewelry.

▲ *Most gemstones have to be cut and polished to be used in jewelry.*

GROWING CRYSTALS

You will need:
- Epsom salts
- measuring cup
- tablespoon
- scissors
- black construction paper
- lid from a large jar

Cut a circle of black paper and fit it inside the jar lid. Fill the measuring cup with 1 cup (237 ml) of water. Add 4 tablespoons (60 ml) of Epsom salts to the water and stir. Pour a thin layer of the mixture into the lid. Let stand for one day without moving it.

Watch the long needle-shaped crystals form on the black paper.

HOT VENTS

Deep under the oceans there are cracks in Earth's crust. These cracks are known as hydrothermal vents. Volcanic activity under the ocean floor causes hot mineral-rich water to shoot out of these vents.

▼ *Chimney-like structures form over hydrothermal vents from the build-up of minerals that escape.*

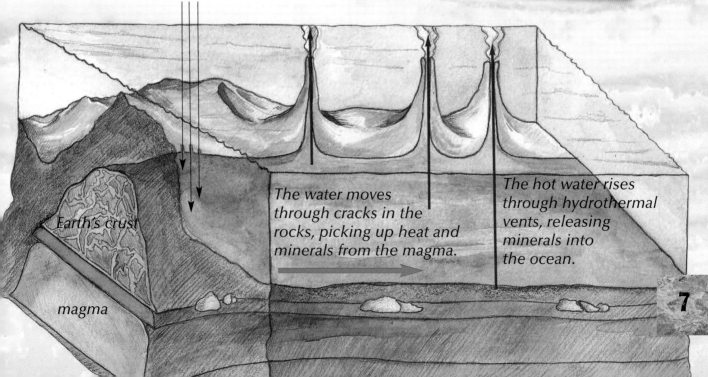

Cold water seeps down through cracks in the ocean floor.

The water moves through cracks in the rocks, picking up heat and minerals from the magma.

The hot water rises through hydrothermal vents, releasing minerals into the ocean.

Earth's crust

magma

ROCK CLASSES

There are almost 4,600 minerals on Earth. With so many minerals, mineralogists needed to organize them into groups. James Dwight Dana (1813–1895) was an American scientist who created a system of organizing minerals into classes based on their elements and structure.

SILLY KATE

Silicates are the largest class of minerals. They all contain silicon and oxygen, but can have a whole range of other elements, too. Quartz and potassium feldspar are two kinds of silicates.

▶ The Dana Classification System created by James Dana is still in use today by mineralogists around the world.

▼ A sample of quartz gold-bearing ore

▼ A sample of potassium feldspar

FANCY CLASS

Sometimes metals combine with oxygen and form the oxide class of minerals. Rare gemstones such as rubies and sapphires belong to this group.

▼ A natural red ruby crystal in feldspar rock

▼ Sapphires come in beautiful shades of blue.

JUST CALL ME YELLOW

Sulfur is a bright yellow element that was used in healing lotions in ancient times. Sulfides are a class of minerals made when sulfur mixes with metals. Pyrite is a sulfide made of sulfur and iron. The sulfate class is created when sulfur mixes with metals and oxygen. The sulfate gypsum is a soft white mineral that we use to make plaster and drywall.

◀ A sample of sulfur

GLITTER AND SHINE

Some minerals are made of only one element that occurs in nature. They are Native minerals and they include diamonds and some metals such as silver and gold.

▼ Silver grains are often used to make jewelry.

▼ Gold nuggets are called "placer gold."

THE OTHERS

Some other classes of minerals are halides, carbonates, and phosphates.

▼ Fluorite is a halide mineral.

▼ Azurite is a carbonate mineral.

▼ Vanadinite is a phosphate mineral.

▼ Examination of Moon soil samples have revealed many similarities to Earth's mineralogy.

IDENTITY ISSUES

Many different minerals share the same shape and color but are not related. Other minerals may look very different from each other but are in the same family. Mineralogists use **luster**, cleavage, fracture, density, hardness, smell, and color to classify and identity minerals.

LUSTER

Luster is the way light bounces off a mineral's surface. Metals like copper are shiny and have a high luster. Gypsum has a silky luster that makes it shimmer.

▼ *Mica is a group of silicates that cleave into perfectly flat sheets.*

BREAK OR CLEAVE

Another way to identify a mineral is by its cleavage or fracture—the way it splits or breaks apart. When a mineral cleaves, it splits into clean flat pieces. Fracturing causes minerals to not break evenly when **struck**.

▼ *The fracture of quartz causes it to have a rough surface when it is broken.*

▼ *Slate cleaves evenly. Slate is mined in quarries and can be used for roof shingles.*

HEAVY WEIGHT

Density can help identify two minerals that look the same. By comparing the weight of two minerals of the same size, scientists can measure which one is denser. A denser mineral weighs more.

▲ *The density of minerals is measured by putting them in water. If a mineral has a density of 2, then it is twice as dense as water.*

SMELLING GOOD

Smell and color are two other properties of minerals that can help identify them. When minerals are heated or struck they often have a strong smell. Color is used to identify minerals that can be only one color, such as malachite, which is green.

◀ *Malachite is a very popular green stone. Its distinctive light and dark green bands make it one of the most easily recognized minerals.*

◀ *Metals like copper have a very high luster.*

STREAK TEST

When minerals are scraped across a white ceramic tile they can leave a mark that helps identify them. This mark is called a streak and is made from the mineral's powder. The streak is not always the same color as the mineral. Cassiterite, a black mineral, leaves a white streak, and brown-black sphalerite makes a yellow streak.

▲ *White ceramic tiles can be used for streak tests.*

SCRATCHED BY MR.MOHS

Scientists discovered that a good way to tell minerals apart is by testing how easy they are to scratch.

ONE TO TEN
Friedrich Mohs was a mineralogist who invented a scale in 1812 to measure the hardness of minerals. All minerals are placed on the scale using a scratch test. The scale rates them from 1 to 10. The softest minerals are 1 and the hardest are 10.

TOUGH DIAMONDS
Mohs identified tools or materials that could be used to scratch minerals at each level, such as fingernails for soft minerals and sandpaper for harder ones. All minerals can scratch minerals that are the same or lower on the scale, but cannot scratch those that are higher. Talc is a 1 on the Mohs scale. Talc is so soft that it is used to make baby powder. Diamonds are a 10 on the scale and can scratch every other mineral on Earth.

GREAT TIPS!

✱ Diamonds are so hard that grains of this mineral are added to the tips of saw blades to slice through rocks, **concrete**, marble, and granite blocks.

▼ *Diamond-tipped saws can cut through thick slabs of granite.*

▼ *Diamonds are the hardest of all minerals.*

MOHS SCALE

DIAMOND
The hardest!
▶ Can be scratched only by another diamond.

10

CORUNDUM
▶ Can be scratched by a diamond.
9

HARDER MINERALS

TOPAZ
▶ Can be scratched by an **emery board.**
8

QUARTZ
▶ Can be scratched by an emerald.
7

FELDSPAR
▶ Can be scratched by a steel file.
6

APATITE
◀ Can be scratched by a steel knife.
5

FLUORITE
◀ Can be scratched by glass.
4

SOFTER MINERALS

CALCITE
◀ Can be scratched by a piece of copper.
3

GYPSUM
◀ Can be scratched by a fingernail with difficulty.
2

TALC
◀ Can be scratched by a fingernail.
The softest!
1

13

COMMON SILICATES

Silicon and oxygen are the two most common elements on Earth. It is not surprising that 90 percent of all minerals are silicates. The most common minerals on Earth are quartz, feldspar, and olivine.

▲ The pure, colorless form of quartz is called rock crystal.

▼ Aquamarine is a blue variety of beryl.

QUARTZ AROUND US

Quartz is found on every continent on Earth. It is a major part of rocks such as granite and gneiss (pronounced "nice"). Almost all the sand in deserts, on beaches, and in sandstone is also quartz. Mountain ranges like the Rocky Mountains, **plateaus** like the Canadian Shield, deserts like the Sahara, and the continent of Antarctica are all made mostly of quartz.

▼ Emerald is a green variety of beryl.

PURE MEANS CLEAR

Quartz comes in many colors. Rock crystal is the name for clear, colorless quartz. Some gemstones that are varieties of the same mineral have different names because of their colors. For example, emerald and aquamarine are both varieties of the silicate mineral called beryl.

CRYSTAL SKULLS

✳ Several quartz rock skull carvings have been found around the world. Some people say the quartz has healing or **supernatural** powers. Scientists are examining these discoveries to find out who might have carved them and when.

▼ *A crystal skull carved from a single piece of quartz.*

◀ *The Sahara desert is mostly made up of quartz sand.*

IS IT AN OLIVE?

Most of Earth's crust is made up of feldspar. This silicate is a little softer than quartz. Earth's mantle, the layer of Earth just under Earth's crust, is made up of liquid rock that contains mostly the mineral olivine. This mineral gets its name from the olive green color it has when it cools.

▼ *Olivine has also been found in meteorites.*

THE NAME GAME

✳ How do minerals get their names? Some are named for the places where they are found. Strontianite was discovered in Strontian, Scotland. Some minerals are named after the people who found them. Livingstonite is named after the famous explorer Dr. David Livingstone.

◀ *Dr. Livingstone is famous for his transcontinental journey across Africa.*

▲ *Sample of livingstonite mineral*

THE PRECIOUS ONES

Most minerals form small, dull crystals. But a few form large, nicely shaped crystals in beautiful colors called gemstones. These gemstones are cut and polished to create gems.

▲ Green emeralds are very valuable gems.

WHAT A GEM!

There are more than 4,500 types of minerals on Earth, but only 160 can form gemstones. The rarest and most beautiful gemstones, such as diamonds, rubies, and sapphires, can be very expensive.

DIAMOND RAINBOW

Diamonds form deep inside Earth under high heat and pressure. While the purest diamonds are clear, many diamonds contain some **impurity** that can make them yellow, orange, green, pink, blue, grey—almost every color in the rainbow!

▶ Red diamonds are the rarest and most exotic diamonds of them all.

NOT AT ANY PRICE

❋ Natural red diamonds are so rare that most people will never even see one. The largest one ever found, called the Moussaieff red diamond, was only about five carats (a little bigger than a raisin). Scientists have not yet discovered what makes red diamonds red.

NOT SO PLAIN

Gemstones often look like plain pebbles until they are cleaned and polished. Lapidarists (gem cutters) use a polishing wheel to polish and cut the stones into different shapes that sparkle. Gemstones are so small that often the work is done under a magnifying glass.

◀ *Raw rubies can be found in other minerals.*

FAKE IT!

Gemstones are valuable because they are hard to find and sometimes hard to get out of rocks. Some people have turned to making artificial gemstones instead. Cubic zirconia "diamonds" look and sparkle like real diamonds.

▼ *Gem cutter using his polishing wheel*

I'VE GOT THE POWER!

❋ Throughout history people have believed that minerals had special powers. Aquamarine was thought to protect sailors at sea. Emeralds were supposed to make people more intelligent. Topaz was believed to give people strength.

▶ *Sailors considered aquamarine to be their lucky stone.*

NOT JUST LUCK ANYMORE

Long ago, finding valuable minerals was often hit or miss. A rock on the ground containing minerals could mean a **deposit** was nearby, or not. Sometimes finding minerals was just luck, such as the gold that sparked the Yukon gold rush. Today, geologists have more scientific ways of finding minerals.

LOCATION, LOCATION, LOCATION

Geologists start by locating areas with the type of rock or landscape where minerals may have formed. **Extinct** volcano fields, ancient seafloors, or old mountain ranges are all places where heat and pressure could have produced certain minerals.

▲ *Geologists often work in remote areas.*

GEOLOGISTS ONBOARD

These areas are then surveyed, or investigated, to check for changes in gravity, magnetism, or **radioactivity**. These changes can signal minerals are under the ground. Geologists sometimes use airplanes or helicopters with special equipment to survey large areas.

▶ *Geologists use helicopters and mobile drilling rigs in their research.*

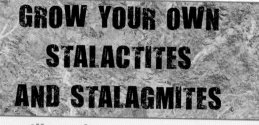

GROW YOUR OWN STALACTITES AND STALAGMITES

You will need:

- Epsom salts
- 2 small jars
  (such as baby food jars)
- cotton string
- scissors
- 2 washers
- spoon
- ruler
- paper

Fill each jar with Epsom salts.

Add water just to the top of the Epsom salts and stir.

Cut a piece of string about 24 inches (61 cm) long.

Tie a washer to each end of the string and place one washer in each jar.

Place a piece of paper between the two jars.

Move the jars so the string hangs between them with the loop about 1 inch above the paper.

Let the jars stand in a still place without touching them for about one week.

GROUND WORK

Scientists take samples of the soil and rocks on the ground, looking for chemicals that may signal the presence of minerals. They also use large drills to take samples from deep under the ground. The samples are then sent to a laboratory to see if and how many minerals may be in the area.

▼ *Drill samples in a storage area*

MINERAL TOWERS

Stalactites and stalagmites are rock formations found in caves. They form when minerals in dripping water begin to collect. Stalactites look like icicles made of stone. Stalagmites are the mineral towers on the ground that grow up to meet the stalactites on the cave's ceiling. Together they form very interesting columns.

▶ *Stalactites and stalagmites form in limestone caves.*

MINING IT

People have been mining minerals for thousands of years. Native North Americans mined copper and used it to make tools. Ancient Europeans combined copper and tin to make a much stronger metal called bronze. Today, there are mines for almost every kind of commercial mineral.

► Coal is often mined in open pits.

DEEP OR SHALLOW

There are two main ways to remove minerals from the Earth. One is open-pit mining and the other is underground mining. The method used depends on how deep the mineral deposit is under the ground.

▼ Gypsum is used in construction.

OPEN WIDE

Open pit mining is used when the mineral is close to the surface. Large machines scrape away the other rocks to expose the mineral-rich rocks. Then miners dig out the rocks with big shovels. Copper, gold, and gypsum are often mined in open pits.

GOING UNDERGROUND

When mineral deposits are too deep for open-pit mining, underground mining is used. Miners dig shafts down into the ground that lead to the minerals. Mining machines dig out the rock, which is sent to the surface on **conveyors**.

▼ *Mining tunnel in an underground mine.*

✳ In the 1990s, diamonds were discovered in northern Canada. Today, there are four Canadian diamond mines using both open pit and underground mining. **Lasers** etch a serial number on each diamond to prove they are from Canadian mines.

▼ *The EKATI Diamond Mine is Canada's first surface and underground diamond mine.*

▶ *The Statue of Liberty in New York is made of bronze.*

MELTING ORES

Ores are minerals that are mined to make metals. To remove the metals from the ore, the ore must be smelted. This process heats the ore in blast furnaces. Temperatures of more than 3,000°F (1,649°C) melt the ore so that the metal can be extracted.

◀ *Blast furnaces are used to produce molten metal.*

MIND THAT MINE

Although mining companies try to minimize damage to the environment, mineral mining can create waste that often pollutes the surrounding areas.

TOXIC WATERS

Bits of ores, minerals, and chemicals left over from mining are called tailings. Mining companies store these in a tailings pond. The water in these ponds can be deadly for birds and animals that come to drink. If the walls of a tailings pond burst, the **toxic** chemicals can also pollute nearby farmland and wells.

▼ *Drinking polluted water can be dangerous for wildlife.*

▼ *Building new roads through wilderness can be very disturbing to wildlife and the environment.*

TOWN ON THE MOVE

✳ The mine near Hibbing, Minnesota, is the world's biggest open pit mine. It covers over 2,000 acres (809 hectares). It is so large that as the mine grew larger, the town of Hibbing had to be moved a few miles to the south.

SO DISTURBING

When mines are built, the surrounding land can be damaged. Roads to the mine site cut through animal habitats and farmland. The noise and **vibrations** from mining can disturb birds and animals.

▼ *Microbes are also used to remove metals from mining wastewater. These tiny creatures absorb the toxins and are then removed, leaving clean water.*

FIX IT!

Massive holes or pits in the ground are left after open-pit mining. Governments now insist that mining companies have a plan to reclaim, or fix, the land once the mine closes.

▼ *Trees planted on the waste heaps of an abandoned mine*

MOLECULES AT WORK

New technologies can clean up some mining wastewater. Scientists are using large molecules that attach to metals in wastewater. Filters can then strain out the metals and leave clean water behind that can flow back into the water supply.

▼ *Aerial view of tailing ponds used for mineral waste in rural Utah*

MINERALS AT HOME

We use minerals every day in our homes, schools, industry, and art. Without minerals we wouldn't have cars, airplanes, or houses. There would be no clocks, batteries, aluminum cans, or even computers. Almost everything on Earth contains minerals.

PRETTY AND USEFUL

Gold, silver, and platinum are used to make jewelry, but that is not all they do. Silver is used to make the batteries we use in cameras, toys, and hearing aids. Gold is so good at **conducting** electricity that it can be found in all kinds of electronics, from cell phones and calculators to televisions.

▶ *Gold in a nugget form*

DATA PLAN

Platinum is used to make new fuel cells in cars to replace gasoline. Platinum is also part of computer hard drives, allowing them to store more data.

◀ *External computer hard drive*

▼ *Platinum can be melted and stored in brick form.*

MINERAL MACHINE

✴ A computer is really one big box of minerals. There are 66 different minerals that make up the average computer, including azurite, quartz, gold, silver, bauxite, and talc.

◀ *Computer processing units function like a computer "brain."*

SCHOOL STUFF

Classrooms would be a very different place without minerals. Blackboards were originally made of slate, a rock made mostly of quartz, and chalk is made of calcium carbonate. New whiteboards also contain minerals in their steel, aluminum, or **porcelain** surfaces. Graphite in a pencil makes the black mark on paper, and the quartz crystal in a clock lets you know when it's time to go home!

▲ *Early blackboards were made of sheets of slate.*

STRONG LIKE A HORSE

Steel is an extremely strong metal made from iron ore. It is used as the frame for buildings, cars, bridges, planes, and skyscrapers.

▲ *Graphite is a soft mineral that is used in pencils.*

▼ *Quartz crystals are used in clocks and watches to keep time.*

▼ *Iron ore's color is often rusty brown.*

▼ *Construction worker resting on steel bars*

LOOK GOOD, FEEL GOOD

Minerals affect every part of our lives, from looking good to feeling good. Art, **cosmetics**, jewelry, and vitamins all include minerals.

PRECIOUS EYES

Through the ages, metals such as copper, bronze, silver, and gold were used to make jewelry and statues. Gemstones were used as decoration on everything from rings, bracelets, and pendants to the eyes of statues and masks, or as decorative patterns on **urns** and coffins.

▶ *Pharaoh Tutankhamen's coffin is made of solid gold and inlaid with gemstones.*

WHAT'S YOUR BIRTHSTONE?

Today, many gemstones and crystals have special meanings. Each month has a birthstone connected with it. Diamonds are also the traditional gem for engagement and wedding rings.

▶ *Most gemstones have to be cut and polished to look beautiful.*

SMILE!

Make your own toothpaste:

You will need:

- ½ tsp (2 ml) calcium carbonate
- ¼ tsp (1 ml) sodium bicarbonate (baking soda)
- water
- plastic spoons
- eye dropper
- small plastic cup
- stick for stirring
- assorted food colors and flavoring
- optional items: fluoride (to prevent cavities), sugar (for taste), diatomite (mild abrasive)

Mix the calcium carbonate and sodium bicarbonate in a small plastic cup with just enough water to make a paste. Add food coloring and/or flavoring with the eye dropper and add optional items a little bit at a time until you get the desired look and taste.

PRETTY FACES

Makeup has changed a lot since it was first used in ancient civilizations. Egyptians used minerals such as lead, sulfur, and chalk, combined with plant and animal materials in their cosmetics. Today, makeup is made with minerals that are thought to be healthy for the skin. Titanium dioxide helps to block harmful rays from the Sun and kaolin soaks up oils.

▶ *Milk is a great source of calcium.*

THE RIGHT BALANCE

Minerals are very important in keeping our bodies healthy. Calcium helps keep bones and teeth strong. Magnesium and potassium are important for our muscles and nerves. These minerals are absorbed into plants and when we eat a well balanced diet, we get the minerals we need.

▼ *Minerals in food help your body grow, develop, and stay healthy.*

27

SO AMAZING

Some minerals have amazing **properties**! They can be see-through, fluorescent, and even magnetic. Some minerals are so rare that only a few crystals have ever been found.

GET A LODE OF THIS!

A lodestone is a naturally magnetic piece of the mineral magnetite. Thousands of years ago, people noticed how a piece of this mineral would always move to point north. Lodestone artifacts have been found in Mexico and China where scientists believe they were used to make the first compasses.

▲ *Crystals in magnetite act like tiny compass needles lining up with Earth's magnetic field.*

▼ *The magnetic compass was invented during the Chinese Han Dynasty between 206 BC and 220 AD.*

TV TUBES

Ulexite is known as the TV rock. Its fibers act like tubes, sending light from one side to the other, so any image under the mineral is shown on the surface, just like an old TV screen.

◀ *Ulexite appears as silky white crystalized masses or parallel fibers.*

◀ *Prospectors often search for scheelite at night with ultraviolet lamps.*

▶ *Opals are gemstones that shimmer in many colors.*

MYSTERIOUS GLOWS

Fluorescent minerals glow in the dark. Scheelite normally has a brilliant blue color under ultraviolet light. Some uranium minerals have a greenish yellow color. Other minerals become fluorescent when they contain other elements such as lead and manganese. Calcite can glow red, green, bright blue, or pink.

IS IT TRUE?

Opals are not true minerals—they are called mineraloids because they do not form crystals. They are related to quartz and their structure makes them bend light so that they shimmer in a rainbow of colors.

THE RAREST OF THEM ALL

Painite was once thought to be the rarest mineral on Earth. It was first found in Myanmar in the 1950s. By 2005, there were only 25 known crystals of painite. Lately, new sources of the orange-red mineral have been discovered.

◀ *Painite is a very rare borate mineral.*

GLOSSARY

analyzing To discover something through examination

bond To be joined securely to something else

classes A group or set of things having something in common

concrete A construction material made of cement, gravel, and water

conducting Moving a form of energy such as electricity or heat

continent One of the seven main landmasses on Earth, such as North America

conveyor A moving belt that transports things

cosmetics A product applied to the body to make it look better

deposit A layer of material that has built up over time

emery board A piece of cardboard with a strong, rough surface

extinct No longer surviving or active, as in an animal species or a volcano

gem A gemstone that has been cut and polished to reveal its beauty

gemstone A mineral, rock, or organic material that is used for jewelry and ornaments

impurity A material that should not be there

lasers A very strong beam of light

luster A soft glow

plateaus High, level ground

porcelain A ceramic material made of clay

properties Characteristics

radioactive Something that gives off radiation

struck Hit very hard

supernatural Something outside of our laws of nature

toxic Poisonous

urn A vase used for holding the remains of a deceased person or animal

vibration Continuous, fast shaking

MORE INFORMATION

FURTHER READING

Minerals.
Morganelli, Adrianna. Crabtree Publishing, 2004.

Everything Rocks and Minerals: Dazzling gems of photos and info that will rock your world!
Tomecek, Steve. National Geographic Children's Books, 2011.

Explore Rocks and Minerals!
Light Brown, Cynthia and Nick Brown. Nomad Press, 2010.

100 Facts on Rocks and Minerals.
Callery, Sean. Miles Kelly Publishing Ltd., 2009.

WEBSITES

The Mineralogical Society of America: Mineralogy for Kids:
www.mineralogy4kids.org/

Rocks for Kids:
www.rocksforkids.com/

Rocks and Minerals 4 U:
www.rocksandminerals4u.com/

Kids Konnect: Rocks and Minerals
www.kidskonnect.com/subject-index/15-science/97-rocks-a-minerals.html

INDEX